# Table of Contents

# INTRODUCTION
## A WORD FROM MARILYN

As you read these stories of children in the Bible, I pray you will be inspired and encouraged by the victories recorded here. You will see that, although times and cultures change, God's *unchanging* Word has an answer for every problem and circumstance. Each example from the Bible demonstrates that the Word will never fail anyone who stands firm on God's promises.

Take the Word into every situation, and be an overcomer. Today you may need divine instruction and intervention in one or more areas of your life. You, or another, may need healing, deliverance, a financial breakthrough, or a relationship reconciled. Let me assure you, the Lord can redeem every situation!

Preserved in the pages of the Bible are victorious accounts of people's lives. Relive these stories with me through this booklet, and let faith rise for *your* occasion. You *will* triumph in Christ Jesus!

*"Now all these things happened unto them for ensamples: and they are written for our admonition, . . . "* (I Corinthians 10:11).

1

*"Now thanks be unto God, which always causeth us to triumph in Christ, and maketh manifest the savour of his knowledge by us in every place"* (II Corinthians 2:14).

His love and mine,

*Marilyn*

# JESUS
## (Luke 2:41-52)

The young lad looked like any other boy who played in the dusty streets of Israel; there was nothing to call one's attention to Him. He was simply one of thousands who flooded Jerusalem for the Passover Feast. The boy and His parents had traveled about a hundred miles from their hometown of Nazareth to be in the Holy City for the great feast. Here the air was filled with excitement, and everywhere tantalizing sights and smells greeted the passerby.

But twelve-year-old Jesus was not looking at the many tempting items for sale on the carts that lined the streets; He was in the Temple talking to the scribes and scholars of Israel. Jesus, with His brothers and sisters, had entered the Temple with Mary and Joseph who came there to present their sacrifice. Losing Himself in the crowd, Jesus had lingered behind, unnoticed, when His family left.

Jesus approached one of the priests and spoke to him. Startled by the profound question asked by the young lad, the priest searched for an answer. While he pondered the matter, Jesus offered an answer that was even more startling than the question. "Why didn't I think of that," thought the priest, "where did this child learn such wisdom?"

Later, noticing the boy talking to a scribe, several other scribes and teachers of the law joined the pair. Jesus continued to ask questions, astonishing the men with His avid interest in matters that seldom troubled the minds of most twelve year olds. For three days Jesus was literally the center of attention. He listened with keen attention to the scribes and teachers, and His comments showed a revelation of wisdom and understanding far beyond His years.

When Jesus' worried parents finally found Him among the teachers, they were astonished. Mary exclaimed, "Son, why have You treated us this way? Your father and I have searched everywhere for You!" But Jesus added to their consternation by quietly answering, "Why is it that you were looking for Me? Did you not know that I had to be in My Father's house?" Nevertheless, Jesus accompanied His family back to Nazareth and continued to be in submission to His earthly parents. As our young Lord grew, He continued to increase in wisdom; and His kind, gentle ways gave Him favor with both God and the people around Him.

Little is known of Jesus' early childhood, but this incident clearly illustrates His interest in God and His desire to apply Himself to learning. Your children, too, have a God-given hunger and ability to acquire knowledge and learn about the Lord. With encouragement, instruction, and prayer, even the smallest child can grow intellectually and spiritually just as Jesus did.

# Scriptures for You and Your Children:

*"The fear of the LORD is the beginning of wisdom: a good understanding have all they that do his commandments: his praise endureth for ever"* (Psalms 111:10).

*"For the LORD gives wisdom; From His mouth come knowledge and understanding. He stores up sound wisdom for the upright; . . . "* (Proverbs 2:6,7 NAS).

*"And all thy children shall be taught of the LORD; and great shall be the peace of thy children"* (Isaiah 54:13).

*"That the God of our Lord Jesus Christ, the Father of glory, may give unto you the spirit of wisdom and revelation in the knowledge of him"* (Ephesians 1:17).

# JOSEPH
## (Genesis 30:22-24, 37:39-50)

No one could miss the young teen-age boy as he swaggered down the path in his beautiful coat of brilliant colors. Obviously, he was proud of it. But why was this young man, who was next to the youngest in a large family of boys, wearing such a coat? This garment marked him as the son who was to be the recipient of the family birthright, contrary to established custom which gave the birthright to the eldest son.

Joseph was well aware that Jacob's favoritism made him the brunt of his ten older brothers' anger and jealousy. But didn't he have the right to receive the inheritance? After all, he was the first son of Rachel, his father's favorite wife, and the only one for whom Jacob had bargained. When Rachel died giving birth to a second son, Jacob favored Joseph all the more.

"Today," Joseph thought, "I will prove to my father that I am worthy of the favor he has bestowed upon me." Joseph had been given the authority to shepherd his father's flocks with four of his brothers to help. It was a grave responsibility for a seventeen-year-old boy, and apparently one which his brothers resented. While Joseph worked, the brothers played; and now Joseph was going to report the vagrancy to his father. Needless to say, this did not endear Joseph to his brothers.

To make matters worse, Joseph was a dreamer. He told of a dream in which he and his brothers were binding sheaves in a field, and his brothers' sheaves bowed down to his sheaf. With great sarcasm his brothers replied, "Are you really going to rule over us?" Later, Joseph reported having dreamed the sun, moon, and eleven stars bowed down to him. At this, even Jacob rebuked the "presumptuous" lad.

In spite of all these things, Joseph truly was being dealt with by the Lord, as he was a young person with a real heart for God. God has a way of making things work out well for those who put Him first, regardless of all the difficulties. And for Joseph, things got decidedly worse.

Making the most of an opportunity, Joseph's brothers plotted to kill him. However, Reuben, the oldest, sensing some responsibility for Joseph's life, talked his other brothers out of murder. Instead, they stripped Joseph of his beautiful coat, dipped it in animal blood, and reported Joseph's death to his anguished father.

With little or no conscience, these cruel brothers sold Joseph to a passing caravan on its way to

Egypt where Joseph would undoubtedly be sold into slavery. Away from his father's favor, stripped of all his privilege and position, Joseph had only the Lord on Whom to rely. Joseph didn't fail the Lord, and the Lord did not fail Joseph.

By the time Joseph was thirty years old, he was Pharaoh's right-hand man, with all the prestige and responsibility such a position commanded. How did this happen? Well, it didn't come easily; but it did come through diligence toward men and faithfulness toward God. Joseph endured slavery, the ruining of his reputation, and even prison—but through it all, Joseph was an overcomer.

Overcomers are never overlooked by God. When God gave Pharaoh a troubling dream, He also gave Joseph the interpretation and put the two of them together. Full of God's wisdom, Joseph not only interpreted the dream but suggested a plan to save Egypt from famine. Pharaoh realized Joseph's worth and set him in a position where he could carry out the plan. In one day's time, a slave became a ruler because he was true to God in every circumstance.

Parents, beware of playing favorites with your children. Put the Lord first, and make every effort to keep strife out of your home. Develop an atmosphere of love and respect where each child is valued as precious to you and to God. If you have failed in these areas, repent and let the Holy Spirit take control. Although Jacob made mistakes, he nurtured a love for God in the heart of his son. When Joseph was later reunited with his family, he could say to his brothers, "It was not you who sent me here, but God. You thought evil against me; but God meant it for good." (See Genesis 45:4-8.)

## Scriptures for You and Your Children:

*"For thou, LORD, wilt bless the righteous; with favour wilt thou compass him as with a shield"* (Psalms 5:12).

*" . . . the seed of the righteous shall be delivered"* (Proverbs 11:21).

*"A wrathful man stirreth up strife: but he that is slow to anger appeaseth strife"* (Proverbs 15:18).

*" . . . jealousy is cruel as the grave: the coals thereof are coals of fire, which hath a most vehement flame. Many waters cannot quench love, neither can the floods drown it: . . . "* (Song of Solomon 8:6,7).

# MIRIAM
## (Exodus 2:1-10)

Breathlessly the young girl waited, keeping a careful eye on the little basket which gently bobbed up and down on the surface of the water. Peeking through the bulrushes along the river bank, Miriam watched to see what would happen next. The girl's heart leaped with anticipation when she saw the beautiful lady part the reeds and step into the water near where Miriam had placed the basket. Accompanied by her maids, the princess of Egypt had come to the river to bathe.

Pharaoh's daughter immediately spotted the strange-looking object intruding her private bathing area. Before taking another step, she pointed to the basket and ordered, "Bring that to me." One of the maids was prompt to obey, and soon she stood before the princess holding the basket in her arms.

Curiously the princess reached out and pulled back the cloth that covered whatever was concealed in the basket. Her eyes grew wide as she sucked in her breath in amazement. Startled, the princess drew back, and for an instant she was speechless. Tucked inside the basket, ever so carefully, was a small baby, who now began to cry.

Miriam heard Pharaoh's daughter exclaim, "This is one of the Hebrew children!" Without a moment's hesitation, Miriam bravely stepped from her hiding place. The situation was tense, but Miriam relaxed a bit when she saw the look of compassion on the princess' face. The Hebrew baby already had wrapped himself around the heart of the childless woman, who envisioned herself raising the abandoned child as her own. "I will call him Moses," announced the princess, "because he was drawn out of the water."

The princess was so intent on the bundle which she now held that she had scarcely noticed the girl who suddenly appeared from nowhere. Mustering all her courage, Miriam seized this advantage and stepped closer. Then she spoke. "Shall I go and call a nurse for you from the Hebrew women, that she may nurse the child for you?"

"How unusual that such an opportunity should be afforded me," thought the princess. Aloud, she said, "Yes, please do that. Take the child and see that he is nursed. I will give you your wages; and when he is weaned, bring him back to me." Miriam jubilantly took her little brother to his own mother who had the miraculous privilege of nurturing her son physically AND spiritually during the formative years of his life.

11

Such a preposterous and impossible situation! Only God could do a thing like that because of the faith of a godly couple and a courageous little girl who refused to surrender their precious son and brother to Pharaoh's evil will. When Egypt's ruler had come to fear the numerical strength of his Hebrew slaves, he sent out a decree that all their male infants should be drowned in the Nile.

How ironic that Pharaoh's own daughter should rescue this Hebrew infant from his hiding place on the very waters in which he was supposed to die. Pharaoh's daughter raised Moses as her own and educated him to be the next pharaoh. Unknowingly, she was doing the will of Almighty God by preserving the future deliverer of Israel.

There is never a circumstance or difficulty that cannot be overruled by God. In this day when all Satan's vengeance seems to be focused on your children, it is encouraging to know that even the actions of a young girl could outsmart the devil when she exercised courage and faith. Program your sons and daughters with the Word of God and defeat Satan's program. See your children as strong and courageous in the Lord Jesus Christ.

# Scriptures for You and Your Children:

*"Have not I commanded thee? Be strong and of a good courage; be not afraid, neither be thou dismayed: for the LORD thy God is with thee whithersoever thou goest"* (Joshua 1:9).

*". . . but as for me and my house, we will serve the LORD"* (Joshua 24:15).

*"Wait on the LORD: be of good courage, and he shall strengthen thine heart: wait, I say, on the LORD"* (Psalms 27:14).

*"For God hath not given us the spirit of fear; but of power, and of love, and of a sound mind"* (II Timothy 1:7).

# ISAAC
## (Genesis 21:1-7, 22:1-18)

The lovely woman smiled with pleasure at the newborn baby whom she held in her arms. Although an older lady, she was strikingly beautiful; and at this moment she literally glowed. Looking into the face of the old man standing beside her, Sarah spoke, "After all these years, who would ever have thought your wife would give birth to a child?"

Abraham chuckled with pride at the two before him. His eyes revealed the awe and wonder in his soul. Sarah continued to speak, "God has turned the shame of my barrenness into joy and replaced my tears with laughter. Everyone who hears of this will join me in laughter." After reflecting a moment, she said, "Now I see, Abraham, why the Lord told you to name our son Isaac meaning laughter."

Obviously, this was no ordinary birth. Here was a miracle baby, born after all possibility of this couple becoming parents was past. But Abraham and Sarah's son was a child of God's promise, proof that God always keeps His Word. Isaac would be the line through whom Messiah would come.

Twenty-five years had passed from the time the

Lord first appeared to Abraham with the promise of multiple blessings which included this son. When all hope of being able to produce any offspring was gone, Abraham had continued to believe God's Word. Abraham had given much thought to those words which inspired him to hope only in the Lord God Almighty.

God had chosen Abraham because he was a man of faith and because he would teach the ways of the Lord to his offspring. Entering a blood covenant relationship with Abraham, the Lord pledged Himself to this man and all his generations. God and Abraham were committed to each other; everything that was Abraham's was God's, and everything that was God's was Abraham's.

The day came when Abraham had to prove his commitment. God asked Abraham to sacrifice Isaac, the one through whom the covenant blessings were to be fulfilled. Abraham purposed to obey, certain that God Who had given life to Isaac, would give life to him a second time. Not until Isaac was on the altar did God intervene. God, alone, would be required to sacrifice His spotless Son for the sin of mankind.

Isaac is often overlooked in this real-life drama. Faith was alive in the young man's heart, too, because he was trained in the Word of God. In His infinite wisdom, God had foreseen the day when the sacrifice of His own Son lay in the balance; and He had entered into a covenant with a man who would teach faith to his son. When Isaac realized he was to be the sacrifice, there was no struggle. Isaac willingly agreed, knowing that God would keep His promise with a miraculous provision.

Every child is a blessing from God, unique and full of promise. The Lord wants each one of them. You as a parent have the God-given responsibility of training your children in the way of the Lord, knowing that they will not depart from it. The Lord has given gifts and talents to your children which will come to fruition when their hearts are full of the Word. Consecrate yourself and your children to God, and allow them to become the blessings God intended.

# Scriptures for You and Your Children:

*"Commit thy way unto the LORD; trust also in him; and he shall bring it to pass"* (Psalms 37:5).

*"But the mercy of the LORD is from everlast-*

*ing to everlasting upon them that fear him, and his righteousness unto children's children; To such as keep his covenant, and to those that remember his commandments to do them"* (Psalms 103:17,18).

*"Train up a child in the way he should go: and when he is old, he will not depart from it"* (Proverbs 22:6).

*"Children, obey your parents in the Lord: for this is right. Honour thy father and mother; which is the first commandment with promise; That it may be well with thee, and thou mayest live long on the earth. And, ye fathers, provoke not your children to wrath: but bring them up in the nurture and admonition of the Lord"* (Ephesians 6:1-4). (See Colossians 3:20,21.)

# JOHN THE BAPTIST
## (Luke 1,2)

Elizabeth stood looking out the window—not really seeing the images before her. Her mind's eye was caught away in the wonder of events that had transpired over the last few months. The light streaming through the window silhouetted the rounded figure of the woman. Elizabeth glanced down at her stomach which could no longer be hidden by the folds of her dress. A warm shiver of delight coursed through her body at the very thought of carrying the child she never expected to have.

Speaking aloud to herself, Elizabeth said, "This is the marvelous way the Lord has dealt with me when He looked upon me with favor." Elizabeth vividly recalled the day, six months earlier, when Zacharias had come home from his priestly duties in the Temple—speechless from his encounter with an angel. Not one word had passed Zacharias' lips from that moment, and his only means of communication was writing.

It was while Zacharias was in the Holy Place before the altar of incense that the angel had suddenly appeared to him. Fear gripped the old

18

priest. He listened in disbelief to Gabriel's words, "Do not be afraid, Zacharias! Your petition has been heard; your wife Elizabeth will bear you a son, whom you are to name John. This child will bring joy and gladness to you, and many will rejoice at his birth. But your doubt has caused you to be *dumb* until the child is born."

Elizabeth still stood at the window wondering what the Lord had in store for the precious life she now carried, when she became aware of the slight figure of a young woman climbing the hill to her home. "Why, that looks like cousin Mary," exclaimed Elizabeth. "It is Mary! What a delightful time for her to come; what a marvelous blessing I have to share with this sweet girl." Elizabeth opened the door, and the two women fell into one another's arms.

The embrace ended, and Elizabeth and Mary looked lovingly at each other. Mary spoke the first word of greeting. Instantly Elizabeth felt her baby leap within her, and she was overwhelmed with joy. At that moment an amazing revelation broke upon her spirit, and she began to prophesy, "Blessed among women are you, and blessed is the fruit of YOUR womb. My baby leaped for joy at your greeting! How has it happened that the mother of my Lord should come to me?"

It was then Mary's turn to speak words of

prophecy. "My soul exalts the Lord, and my spirit has rejoiced in God my Savior, because He has regarded the humble state of His maidservant. The mighty One has done great things for me; and holy is His name. His mercy is upon generation after generation toward those who fear Him!" Mary continued to extol the wondrous works of God toward His people.

When Mary had finished, Elizabeth stood staring at her, while her mind caught up with the words they had both spoken. Here before her stood the mother of Judah's long-awaited Messiah, the deliverer of Israel! Strange circumstances also surrounded this child's conception. Elizabeth listened as Mary told of another angelic visitation three months earlier. Mary, too, had been stunned at Gabriel's announcement; but she trusted the Lord. Mary was to bear God's Son!

"You well know," Mary said, "that Joseph and I were not yet wed. The angel assured me that nothing was impossible to God and told me the child would be conceived of the Holy Ghost while I was still a virgin. The angel also made a visit to Joseph, and he and I have quietly married. Joseph sent me here to spend some time with you." The two women embraced again and marvelled at how *each* of their worlds had been suddenly and wonderfully invaded by God.

A few months later when Elizabeth gave birth to a son, Zacharias' tongue was loosed; and he joyfully told everyone the baby's name was John. Little John was carefully and lovingly nurtured by his parents in the things of God. John loved to hear his parents tell the story of his miraculous birth, and he purposed in his heart to serve the Lord all the days of his life. It was John whom God used to proclaim the good news that Mary's Son Jesus was the Lamb of God sent to redeem the world from sin.

Mom and Dad, your children, too, have been given a very special life by our loving God. The Lord had each of them in mind when He sent His Son to bring salvation to the earth. No doubt, you have marvelled at the miracle of your children's birth and at the awesome responsibility of raising them. Never forget, it is your commitment to the Lord and the godly training you give each child which will reap joyful results. Gabriel's words to Mary are still true today, "Nothing is impossible with God!"

# Scriptures for You and Your Children:

"... With men this is impossible; but with God all things are possible" (Matthew 19:26).

"Jesus said unto him, If thou canst believe, all things are possible to him that believeth" (Mark 9:23).

"And his mercy is on them that fear him from generation to generation" (Luke 1:50).

"... we being delivered out of the hand of our enemies might serve him without fear, In holiness and righteousness before him, all the days of our life" (Luke 1:74,75).

# JOSIAH
## (II Kings 11)

Jehosheba held her breath as the queen's private guard searched the house. A wave of nausea flooded over her as she thought about the events of this awful day. "I must not faint," she thought, "the life of the young prince depends on me." A mental picture of the evil woman Athaliah flashed across Jehosheba's mind. "How could she do this wicked thing," thought Jehosheba aloud, "and to her own grandchildren?"

The last few days in Judah had been tumultuous ones, indeed. King Ahaziah had been killed, and now his power-hungry mother was having all her son's children murdered in order that she could have the throne. Jehosheba, realizing what was happening, had hidden the youngest son and his nurse in a bedroom. After the guard finished the search, Jehosheba breathed a sigh of relief. "O Lord," she prayed, "spare this little one. Please keep Athaliah from inquiring about the infant. The men will surely not think of him."

The prayer of this godly woman was answered, and for six years Jehosheba lived in the house of the Lord with young prince Josiah. Their presence was known only to a few trusted persons. Meanwhile, the tyrannical Athaliah reigned in Judah. The godless woman was the widow of wicked King Jehoram and the daughter of King Ahab and Queen Jezebel of Israel. Athaliah desecrated the land with idolatry—learning nothing from the tragic end of her mother and father.

A faithful underground of people, led by Jehoiada the priest, had waited and planned for an opportune time to crown Josiah king and to rid Judah of the scourge of Athaliah. Finally the day arrived; the air was charged with excitement! Military captains and their men were stationed at strategic points to see that the coup was carried out successfully. "Keep watch over the Lord's house, and protect the king," Jehoiada commanded. "Put to death anyone who comes within your ranks."

At the appointed hour, Jehoiada led Josiah outside the Temple and placed the crown upon his head. Gratefully and reverently Jehoiada handed Josiah the written testimony of God's Word. The group could keep silent no longer. As the trumpets sounded, the people clapped and shouted for joy. "Long live the king," cried the people, "Long live the king!"

Hearing the tumultuous crowd, Athaliah looked

outside to see a boy standing at the Temple porch wearing the crown. Athaliah wasted no time in reaching the scene. "Treason! Treason!" screamed the frenzied woman as she ran across the courtyard in front of the Temple. Surprises were not over for Athaliah; the soldiers were waiting for her. Swiftly these men grasped the screaming woman and carried her forcibly to the door of the palace where they put a quick end to the wicked queen.

Seven years old—and king! But those short years had not been wasted. Josiah had been laboriously tutored in the Word of God and skillfully trained to take the throne. The events of that coronation day were forever etched in Josiah's memory. He never forgot how the people went to the house of Baal, broke the altars and images, and killed the priest of Baal. Nor did Josiah ever forget the covenant which Jehoiada made between the Lord, the king, and the people, when he and all Judah purposed to serve the Lord.

Parents, be diligent in training your children in the Word of God. They are never too young to grasp Biblical principles geared to their level of learning. Even simple songs about Jesus, sung to a babe in arms, are not wasted on an impressionable soul. Little ones are particularly sensitive to spiritual things. Set a godly example for your children at all times, so that your word and your actions agree; they will follow in your footsteps.

# Scriptures for You and Your Children:

*"Shew me thy ways, O LORD; teach me thy paths. Lead me in thy truth, and teach me: for thou art the God of my salvation; on thee do I wait all the day"* (Psalms 25:4,5).

*"For thou art my hope, O Lord GOD: thou art my trust from my youth. By thee have I been holden up from the womb: thou art he that took me out of my mother's bowels: my praise shall be continually of thee"* (Psalms 71:5,6).

*"O God, thou hast taught me from my youth: and hitherto have I declared thy wondrous works"* (Psalms 71:17).

*"REMEMBER now thy Creator in the days of thy youth, while the evil days come not, . . . Fear God, and keep his commandments: for this is the whole duty of man"* (Ecclesiastes 12:1,13).

# SAMUEL
## (I Samuel 1-3)

Hannah prayed so softly the words could not be heard. Her occasional sobs scarcely broke the silence. Hannah was completely unaware of the priest who stood watching her. When the man finally spoke, Hannah was startled by the priest's gruff voice—but his words were even more startling. Hannah asked the priest to repeat himself, but even then the words made no sense. "Drunk! How can he possibly think I'm drunk," Hannah thought.

This godly woman was so shocked by the priest's accusation that it took her a moment to reply. "Oh no, my lord," Hannah exclaimed, "I have not been drinking! But I am so depressed, I have been pouring out my soul to God." Eli listened intently as Hannah continued. "Please do not think me a worthless woman. Although moved with emotion, I am simply speaking to the Lord about a deep hurt that consumes me."

The priest was touched by the woman's intensity and also by her sincere manner. There was no doubt in his mind now that she was *not* drunken. "My dear lady," said Eli, "may I ask the nature of this great concern." Hannah quickly responded by telling Eli of her desire to have a child, a son to present to God and to her beloved husband Elkanah.

Anointed by the Lord, the priest spoke words that encouraged Hannah to believe for a child, so she was no longer sad. Hannah rolled the words over in her mind. "Go in peace, and may God grant your petition," he had said. Hannah nearly skipped as she rose and left the Tabernacle. Indeed, Hannah's heart did skip because she knew God had honored her fasting and prayer.

The months passed quickly, and soon Hannah cradled the child she had so earnestly desired. No longer did she have to bear the shame of barrenness; no longer was she the brunt of the sarcastic remarks of Peninnah, Elkanah's other wife. In spite of the love and attention Elkanah showered on Hannah, she had not been satisfied until the Lord opened her womb and gave her Elkanah's son. Praise to God welled up in Hannah until she thought she might burst.

From the very beginning Hannah knew little Samuel belonged completely to the Lord. Even before his birth, Samuel's mother had purposed in her heart to take her young son to live at the Tabernacle. There he would be God's servant. Never did a doubt enter Hannah's mind about

Samuel's willingness to serve the Lord. To that end, Hannah diligently and faithfully taught Samuel about God and His Word.

After three or four years, Samuel was weaned, and Hannah and Elkanah took him to the Tabernacle. They had done their job well, and a love for God was already instilled in the heart of the child. With joy and thanksgiving, Hannah and Elkanah dedicated Samuel to God and presented him to Eli the priest. It took great faith for Hannah to entrust this special son to the care of another, but she knew Samuel was really in the Lord's care.

Although Eli had failed as a father in his own household, he nurtured his young charge in godly ways. Eli gave to Samuel the discipline and training he was unwilling to give his own spoiled sons, and Samuel grew in favor with the Lord. Even though a word from God was rare in that day, Samuel was still a youth when God first spoke to him.

While Samuel slept, God called, "Samuel, Samuel!" Thinking it was Eli, Samuel ran to the priest who wisely instructed the boy to recognize the Lord's voice. From that time on, Samuel was God's faithful spokesman to Israel. Sometimes the words were tragic, as they were that first night when God foretold the fall of Eli's house, but always they were true. Through it all, this prophet of God was

an instrument of encouragement to the people as
he gave God's message of hope and love.

To the "natural" eye it seemed foolish for
Hannah to have relinquished her precious son to
be raised by a failure! But Hannah had placed
Samuel in God's hands, and He did not fail her.
No matter what the circumstances, you mothers
and fathers can mark your children for God, just
as Hannah did. Rest assured that they will come
through for God in spite of bad surroundings, peer
pressure, or worldly temptations. Stand on the
promises of God, and He will not let you down.

## Scriptures for You and Your Children:

*"And Hannah prayed, and said, My heart
rejoiceth in the LORD; mine horn is exalted in the
LORD: my mouth is enlarged over mine enemies;
because I rejoice in thy salvation"* (I Samuel 2:1).

*"He [God] raiseth up the poor out of the dust,
and lifteth up the beggar from the dunghill, to set
them among princes, and to make them inherit
the throne of glory: for the pillars of the earth are
the LORD'S, and he hath set the world upon them"*
(I Samuel 2:8).

*"Trust in the LORD with all thine heart; and*

30

*lean not unto thine own understanding. In all thy ways acknowledge him, and he shall direct thy paths. Be not wise in thine own eyes: fear the LORD, and depart from evil"* (Proverbs 3:5-7).

*"And let us not be weary in well doing: for in due season we shall reap, if we faint not"* (Galatians 6:9).

# DAVID
## (I Samuel 17:4-49)

What a frightening and awesome sight! The giant was over nine-feet tall, and he was clothed from head to foot in heavy metal armor. Lifting his enormous spear over his head, the Philistine giant shouted, "I defy the ranks of Israel this day; give me a man that we may fight together."

Day after day the same thing occurred, while all the fighting men of Israel cowered in fear. If Goliath killed the man sent out to fight with him, Israel would have to surrender to her enemies. BUT, if any man of Israel should slay the giant, the Philistines would become captive to Israel. The odds were ridiculous. The Philistines couldn't possibly lose—or could they?

Goliath's taunt still hung in the air when a handsome young lad of perhaps sixteen stepped into the field that divided the Philistines and the Israelites. Surely this *boy* couldn't be Israel's champion! Goliath watched with a mixture of scorn and anger. He was highly insulted. "I would rather slay a skilled warrior, a leader," muttered Goliath to himself, "but if this is what they choose to send me, the taking will be easy."

No intelligent rationale would have picked the boy to combat the giant. Only the Holy Spirit could have persuaded King Saul and his army to allow David to fight Goliath. But David had been persuasive, "I have killed a bear and a lion with my bare hands," he told the king. Besides, no other soldier had the courage to step into the battle arena, not even Saul.

Had Goliath seen David just minutes before, his anger might have turned to amusement. David had stood before several of Saul's chief warriors—clothed in Saul's armor which was several sizes too big for him. When David tried to walk, he could scarcely move. David laid down Saul's sword, then, slowly and deliberately, took off each piece of the armor. "I cannot go with these, for I have not tested them," David remarked.

Instead, David marched onto the field clothed in all the might and power of God. For a weapon David chose his sling, with which he was an exceedingly accurate marksman. Walking by the brook he stooped down to pick up five small, smooth stones, very carefully chosen. Now David was prepared to face even the devil himself. David was absolutely certain he would slay this enemy of Israel and take his head to the king. Hadn't the Lord promised victory for His people?

Momentarily the two stood and eyed each other across the field, then David started walking toward the big Philistine. Goliath stepped forward with his shield bearer. With a booming voice he yelled, "By my gods! Am I a dog that you come to me with sticks? Come closer, and I will give your flesh to the birds of the sky and the beasts of the field."

With disconcerting calm David replied, "You come to me with a sword, a spear, and a javelin, but I come to you in the name of the Lord of hosts, the God of the armies of Israel, Whom you have taunted. This day the Lord will deliver you into my hands, and I will strike you down and remove your head. Today I will give the dead bodies of the Philistines to the birds and the beasts, that all the earth will know there is a God in Israel. And so that all this group may know the Lord does not deliver by sword or by spear, the Lord will give you into our hands. The battle is the Lord's!"

David stepped to the battle line, took a stone from his bag, and placed it in the sling. With the speed of lightning the stone sped to its target. Before Goliath knew what happened, he slumped to his knees, a sharp pain piercing his forehead. The stone had hit the mark and sunk deeply into his forehead. By the time David reached the fallen giant, he was on his face, all nine feet stretched out on the ground. The final irony came when David took Goliath's own sword and cut off the giant's head. The battle was over, the victory was won!

David went on to become the greatest king in Israel's history, just a boy who knew his God. As a child David had purposed in his heart to serve the Lord; and in spite of some glaring mistakes, he was, nevertheless, "a man after God's own heart."

Train your children in the Word of God, and give them every opportunity in your home to become acquainted with the Lord. They will be champions for God, in spite of whatever mistakes they may make along the way. The power of God's Word will keep them on the right track, and their lives will be lived ultimately in victory.

## Scriptures for You and Your Children:

"Both riches and honour come of thee [O LORD], and thou reignest over all; and in thine hand is power and might; and in thine hand it is to make great, and to give strength unto all" (I Chronicles 29:12).

"O sing unto the LORD a new song; for he hath done marvellous things: his right hand, and his holy arm, hath gotten him the victory. The LORD *hath made known his salvation: his righteousness hath he openly shewed in the sight of the heathen"* (Psalms 98:1,2).

*"O LORD, thou art my God; I will exalt thee, I will praise thy name; for thou hast done wonderful things; thy counsels of old are faithfulness and truth. For thou hast been a strength to the poor, a strength to the needy in his distress, a refuge from the storm, a shadow from the heat, when the blast of the terrible ones is as a storm against the wall"* (Isaiah 25:1,4).

*"For whatsoever is born of God overcometh the world: and this is the victory that overcometh the world, even our faith. Who is he that overcometh the world, but he that believeth that Jesus is the Son of God?"* (I John 5:4,5).

# JAIRUS' DAUGHTER
## (Mark 5:22-43; Luke 8:41-56)

The well-dressed man pushed through the crowd that had gathered along the shore of Galilee and threw himself at Jesus' feet. Obviously in great distress, the man earnestly entreated Jesus, saying, "My little daughter is at the point of death; please, please come, and lay Your hands on her! If You will only come, I know she will get well and live."

Without concern for his position in the synagogue or the opinion of Jesus held by most of his colleagues, Jairus had come to the healer. Not even his emotional display before the crowd kept Jairus from begging for the life of his twelve-year-old child. Jesus was Jairus' only hope, surely He would help. Jesus smiled and began to follow the synagogue official through the crowd. In Jairus' mind there was no time to lose.

To Jairus' dismay, Jesus suddenly stopped and exclaimed, "Who touched My garments?" "O Master," thought Jairus, "anyone in this vast crowd could have touched you. Don't you realize my daughter is dying?" The man's thoughts were verbalized by one of Jesus' disciples who was following along. "You see the multitude pressing in on You, Lord, and You say, 'Who touched Me'?"

A hush came over the people. While Jesus' eyes searched the crowd, a woman stepped forward and fell at His feet sobbing, "I'm healed, I'm healed!" Trembling with fear, the woman told a tragic story of fruitless treatment for a hemorrhage with which she had suffered 12 years. Determined to touch Jesus, she had braved the crowd to receive her reward. Tenderly Jesus said, "Daughter, your faith has made you well; go in peace, and be healed of your affliction."

Jairus' faith, greatly encouraged by this incident, was soon dashed to the ground when his servant came with word of the daughter's death. Overhearing this news, Jesus said to Jairus, "Do not be afraid, only believe! Let us continue to your home." Without hesitation Jairus led the way to the house, accompanied by Jesus and His disciples, Peter, James, and John.

Loud wailing and weeping reached the ears of the five men as they neared the place where Jairus and his family lived. When Jesus arrived at the house, He dismissed the mourners, exclaiming, "Stop weeping, for she has not died, she is asleep!" The people all laughed in scorn, but the stern look on Jesus' face told them they had better leave.

After entering the home, Jairus and his wife led

Jesus to their daughter's still form. Kneeling at the bedside Jesus commanded, "Little girl, I say to you, arise!" Serenely, as though waking from sleep, the child opened her eyes and looked up into the compelling face of the stranger. Jesus grasped the girl's hand, and she arose to her feet completely healed. Overcome with joy, Jairus and his wife watched in astonishment. Without ceremony, Jesus kindly instructed the mother to give her daughter something to eat.

This account should vividly demonstrate to you parents that faith in Jesus is stronger than any problem you may be facing in your family. Faith in God's Word is even stronger than the grip of death itself. When it seems that all is lost, renew your faith with the promises of God, and stand firm. There is no situation that cannot be dismissed by the Word in your heart and in your mouth. You may endure delays, but the Lord will not fail you.

# Scriptures for You and Your Children:

" . . . *I have set before you life and death, blessing and cursing: therefore choose life, that*

*both thou and thy seed may live: That thou
mayest love the L*ORD *thy God, and that thou
mayest obey his voice, and that thou mayest
cleave unto him: for he is thy life, and the length
of thy days: . . . "* (Deuteronomy 30:19,20).

*"Trust in the L*ORD *with all thine heart; and
lean not unto thine own understanding. In all thy
ways acknowledge him, and he shall direct thy
paths"* (Proverbs 3:5,6).

*"For I know the thoughts that I think toward
you, saith the L*ORD, *thoughts of peace, and
not of evil, to give you an expected end"*
(Jeremiah 29:11).

*"So then faith cometh by hearing, and hearing
by the word of God"* (Romans 10:17).

*"Jesus said unto her, I am the resurrection, and
the life: he that believeth in me, though he were
dead, yet shall he live"* (John 11:25).

# TIMOTHY
## (II Timothy 1-4)

"Here's a letter for you," said the messenger as he handed over the small parcel. The young man standing in the doorway took the envelope and quickly broke the seal. With great joy Timothy saw that it was another letter from Paul. Timothy's eyes eagerly raced over the pages like a hungry man gulping food. Then the youthful pastor slowly read and reread the precious message from his old friend, savoring every word and every thought.

Once again Timothy's eyes went back to the beginning of the letter but soon stopped, his mind fixed on these words: "I am mindful of the sincere faith within you, which first dwelt in your Grandmother Lois, and your mother Eunice, and I am sure that it is in you as well." This testimony to Timothy's faith, affirmed by his dear friend and teacher, brought back wonderful memories. A long-forgotten picture formed in Timothy's mind.

A much younger Timothy sat at a woman's feet, gazing intently at the lovely face which was haloed by waves of silver hair. "Please tell me the story again, Grandma," pleaded the boy. "I love to hear how Jesus came back to life after the mean people killed him." Lois needed little coaxing from young Tim to repeat the story of Christ's Resurrection. It delighted the heart of this grandmother to see the eagerness with which her grandson received the Word of God.

There was something special about the telling of the story today, and something special about Timothy's interest. Lois realized the Holy Spirit was nudging the boy to receive Jesus as his own Savior and Lord. When, once again, she finished the story, Lois said, "Do you want to ask Jesus into your heart, Tim?" The child quickly responded to the invitation, and the two bowed their heads in prayer. When young Timothy looked up, his eyes sparkled with tears of joy.

As he recalled that moment when the love of God became so real, tears again formed in Timothy's eyes. "How very blessed I am," thought Timothy, "to have heard the good news of salvation." Timothy's family lived in Greece, hundreds of miles from the land where Jesus had lived, but the gospel message had come to them through an enthusiastic convert. It was Grandmother Lois who first received the Lord Jesus, and she in turn led her daughter Eunice and her grandson Timothy to the Savior.

Although Timothy's father was Greek, his mother and grandmother were Jews, so the lad always had access to the Old Testament scriptures, which he heard and read with great interest. From the day of Timothy's conversion, his only ambition was to become a pastor. The time came when the apostle Paul confirmed the ministry gift in Timothy and faithfully taught his young student. It always touched Timothy's heart to be lovingly referred to as Paul's son in the faith.

The letter, now reverently held in Timothy's hand, was a continuation of his spiritual father's training. Timothy's eyes followed down through the pages as he took to heart Paul's most recent exhortations: "Do not be timid or afraid, because God has given you power, love, and a sound mind"; "be diligent in your study of God's Word"; "refuse foolish and ignorant speculations"; "be kind to all, able to teach, patient when wronged." Many will receive the Lord!

What a privilege you have, mother, father, or grandparent, to teach the Word of God to your little ones. That "seed" planted in their hearts will bear much fruit. Your most important task is the diligent training of these entrusted to you. Don't forget to let these children see you in the Word and in prayer; be a good example for them. If your children are older now, it is never too late to begin. Water the soil with prayer, and be ready to make the most of every opportunity—in LOVE!

# Scriptures for You and Your Children:

*"And all thy children shall be taught of the LORD; and great shall be the peace of thy children"* (Isaiah 54:13).

*"For God hath not given us the spirit of fear; but of power, and of love, and of a sound mind"* (II Timothy 1:7).

*" . . . I am not ashamed: for I know whom I have believed, and am persuaded that he is able to keep that which I have committed unto him against that day"* (II Timothy 1:12).

*"Study to shew thyself approved unto God, a workman that needeth not to be ashamed, rightly dividing the word of truth"* (II Timothy 2:15).

# THE SYROPHENICIAN'S DAUGHTER

## Delivered From Demons
## (Mark 7:26,27)

The mother helplessly stood watching her young daughter snarl and thrash around on the floor. No amount of effort could quiet the girl, and tears filled the woman's eyes as she wrung her hands in grief and frustration. Time and time again the anxious mother had attempted to get close to the writhing figure but to no avail. The woman's hand, blood still dripping from a deep scratch, bore grim evidence of that fact.

"What can I do, oh, what can I do?" the woman questioned. Great sorrow and despair gripped this Syrophenician mother, who had watched her tormented daughter on many such occasions. "The demon will surely kill my child if I can't find some way in which to help her." As the woman was thinking these thoughts, her daughter began to quiet down and gradually the growling and jerking ceased. The mother heaved a great sigh of relief. It was over—this time.

Kneeling next to her daughter, the woman gently

spoke her name. Gazing out of dark, questioning eyes, the girl stopped moaning and simply asked, "Not again?" With her mother's assistance the girl stumbled over to the couch. Still dazed, she slumped down onto the piece of furniture. The mother sat down beside the girl, put her arm around her, and the two sat there for several moments in silence.

The vacant look on the girl's face was slowly replaced with fear. Burying her face in her mother's arms, the girl began to cry. "I'm so scared," she wailed, "I'm so scared!" The mother tried to comfort her daughter, but she felt as frightened as the child. She had done everything she knew how to do; even an exorcist had not helped.

Several days later the Syrophenician woman's neighbor burst through her door—breathless with excitement. "He's here," she exclaimed, "the Galilean is here in the city of Tyre!" "What Galilean?" asked the puzzled woman. The question opened a floodgate; words tumbled over the neighbor's tongue as she tried to explain Who the Jew from Galilee was. In short, He was the teacher, the healer, the One about Whom everyone was talking. Some even said He was the long-awaited, Jewish Messiah.

One word in particular caught the attention of the Syrophenician woman. That word was *healer*!

The woman began to recall stories she had heard of a man in Israel who had unusual powers to heal the sick and deliver those vexed with demons. Some said He had raised the dead. A flicker of hope was kindled in the woman's spirit: perhaps this was the help for which she had cried.

The woman wasted no time. After asking her neighbor where the healer was, she hurried out the door leaving the friend to watch her daughter. When the eager mother found the house where Jesus was staying, she entered and threw herself at the feet of the One Who was holding the attention of everyone in the room. Over and over the woman begged, "Please come, and cast the demon out of my daughter."

After hearing the mother's plea, Jesus answered, "Let Abraham's children be satisfied first. It is not good to take their bread and throw it to gentile dogs." This response was certainly not what the Syrophenician woman had expected, but she refused to be discouraged. Quickly she said, "Yes, Lord, but even the puppies under the master's table feed on the children's crumbs." With great compassion Jesus then said, "Because you have answered with faith and determination, you may go away satisfied; the demon has gone out of your daughter."

Today, you as a parent may face a problem

similar to that of the woman in this story. Perhaps your son or daughter is being tormented by the powers of hell: rebellion, drugs, alcohol, hard rock music, satanism, etc. Take heart! Your situation is not hopeless. Those who are violent with their faith are the ones who receive kingdom promises. Stand firm on God's Word, and don't be moved by the enemy. You will see bondages broken.

# Scriptures for You and Your Children:

*"And wisdom and knowledge shall be the stability of thy times, and strength of salvation: the fear of the LORD is his treasure"* (Isaiah 33:6).

*"And from the days of John the Baptist until now the kingdom of heaven suffereth violence, and the violent take it by force"* (Matthew 11:12).

*"But rather seek ye the kingdom of God; and all these things shall be added unto you. Fear not, little flock; for it is your Father's good pleasure to give you the kingdom"* (Luke 12:31,32).

*"Finally, my brethren, be strong in the Lord, and in the power of his might. Put on the whole armour of God, that ye may be able to stand against the wiles of the devil"* (Ephesians 6:10,11).

# A DEMONIZED GIRL
## Is Delivered
## (Acts 16:16-21)

"These men are servants of the most high God," the young girl cried out. "They proclaim to you the way of salvation. These men are servants . . . ." Over and over the girl yelled to the crowd as she followed the two men through the streets of Philippi. Anyone would have supposed the child was a part of their company, announcing the presence and purpose of the pair. She was very effective in getting the attention of everyone.

The most casual observer would have guessed the men to be foreigners, and probably Jews, because the men of Philippi did not wear beards. Neither would the average citizen of this Macedonian city proclaim the *most high* God; these superstitious people worshiped a multitude of gods. The more curious townsfolk noticed that the daily destination of the two men was the meeting place of those strange few, who talked about a Jew named Jesus Who claimed to be the ONLY God.

At first Paul and Silas marveled at the ingenious way in which the Lord chose to make their presence known among these people. After all, hadn't God led the two missionaries to this place through a vision of a Macedonian man calling to them. God simply used this method to pave the way for the message of salvation.

Usually Paul and Silas paid little attention to the young girl who was their uninvited advertisement. However, on this day, Paul was annoyed by her proclamation. Searching his spirit to find an answer from the Lord, Paul suddenly realized it was not God Who announced the "good news." This slave girl had a spirit of divination and was being used by Satan. But why? The reason came quickly: the devil wanted the Philippians to identify the strangers with a fortune teller and, therefore, to pay no attention to the message which they brought.

Paul motioned to Silas and the two stopped abruptly in their tracks, nearly causing the slave girl to run into them. In that instant, Paul had the opportunity to look directly into the face of the girl. The blazing eyes of a demon glared back at Paul through the eyes of the tormented girl. Startled, the poor girl was suddenly gripped with fear, and she would have run except for Silas' firm grip on her arm.

Speaking forcefully to the demon, Paul said, "In the name of Jesus Christ, I command you to come out of this young woman, NOW!" Without a split-second's hesitation, the demon came out of the girl. Although dazed and fearful, a look of peace flooded over her face. It was then that Paul and Silas realized the girl was not alone. A very angry man stepped from the crowd and demanded an explanation of Paul's action.

Before Paul or Silas knew what was happening, two men seized the pair and dragged them into the marketplace before the city officials. "These men are throwing our city into confusion," accused the two; "they proclaim customs which are unlawful for us to accept or observe." However, the fact of the matter was that these men had been making an enormous profit by using their young slave as a fortune teller. Now that the girl was delivered from the demon, her masters had lost their income and were furious with Paul and Silas.

Because a girl, bound by Satan and slavery, was set free in the name of Jesus, Paul and Silas were imprisoned. Nevertheless, Paul and Silas also were set free by the Lord's miraculous intervention; and they led the jailer and his family to Christ. No prison, either physical or spiritual, has chains so strong that God cannot break them and set the captive free.

Mom or Dad, does it seem that your child is being mastered by Satan? Do you feel bound and helpless in some situation involving your children?

Are all your efforts frustrated? Don't despair! Jesus has given you the power of His name to rebuke Satan's work. Make God's promises sure in your heart; and, in the authority of Jesus' name, declare God's will—His Word—over every circumstance. Victory is yours!

## Scriptures for You and Your Children:

*"And whoso shall receive one such little child in my name receiveth me. But whoso shall offend one of these little ones which believe in me, it were better for him that a millstone were hanged about his neck, and that he were drowned in the depth of the sea"* (Matthew 18:5,6).

*"And these signs shall follow them that believe; In my name shall they cast out devils; they shall speak with new tongues; They shall take up serpents; and if they drink any deadly thing, it shall not hurt them; they shall lay hands on the sick, and they shall recover"* (Mark 16:17).

*"Behold, I give unto you power to tread on serpents and scorpions, and over all the power*

of the enemy: and nothing shall by any means hurt you" (Luke 10:19).

"He that committeth sin is of the devil; for the devil sinneth from the beginning. For this purpose the Son of God was manifested, that he might destroy the works of the devil" (I John 3:8).

# ALL THE CHILDREN OF THE BIBLE

## OLD TESTAMENT CHILDREN

Genesis 3:15
Genesis 4:2
Genesis 4:17
Genesis 4:18
Genesis 4:25,26
Genesis 4:26
Genesis 5:18
Genesis 5:21
Genesis 5:29
Genesis 6:4
Genesis 16:11,12
Genesis 17
Genesis 19:29-38
Genesis 21:3
Genesis 25:20,26
Genesis 29:32
Genesis 29:33
Genesis 29:34

Genesis 29:35
Genesis 30:1-6
Genesis 30:7,8
Genesis 30:9-11
Genesis 30:12,13
Genesis 30:14-18
Genesis 30:19,20
Genesis 30:21
Genesis 30:22-24
Exodus 2:2
Judges 11
Judges 13
Ruth 4:17
I Samuel 1:20
I Samuel 4:19-22
II Samuel 12:24
I Kings 3:16-18
I Kings 11:14-22
I Kings 14:1-20
I Kings 17
II Kings 4:8-37
II Kings 11:2-21
II Kings 12:1,2
II Kings 22

II Kings 23
II Chronicles 34
Isaiah 7:3
Isaiah 8:1-4
Hosea 1:2-4
Hosea 1:6
Hosea 1:8,9

# NEW TESTAMENT CHILDREN

Matthew 1:18-25
Matthew 2:1-12
Matthew 9:18-26
Matthew 15:21-28
Matthew 17:14-21
Mark 5:22-43
Mark 7:24-30
Mark 9:14-20
Luke 1:5-25, 57-80
Luke 8:41-56
Luke 9:37-43
John 4:46-54
John 9:1-20
II Timothy 1:1-6
II Timothy 3:14-17

# Receive Jesus Christ as Lord and Savior of Your Life

The Bible says, "That if thou shalt confess with thy mouth the Lord Jesus, and shalt believe in thine heart that God hath raised him from the dead, thou shalt be saved. For with the heart man believeth unto righteousness; and with the mouth confession is made unto salvation" (Romans 10:9,10).

To receive Jesus Christ as Lord and Savior of your life, sincerely pray this prayer from your heart:

Dear Jesus,

I believe that You died for me and that You rose again on the third day. I confess to You that I am a sinner and that I need Your love and forgiveness. Come into my life, forgive my sins, and give me eternal life. I confess You now as my Lord. Thank You for my salvation!

Signed _____

Date _____

**Write to us.** We will send you information to help you with your new life in Christ. Marilyn Hickey Ministries • P.O. Box 17340 • Denver, CO 80217.

## BOOKS BY MARILYN HICKEY

A CRY FOR MIRACLES ($5.95)
ACTS ($7.95)
ANGELS ALL AROUND ($7.95)
BEAT TENSION ($.75)
BIBLE CAN CHANGE YOU, THE ($12.95)
BOLD MEN WIN ($.75)
BREAK THE GENERATION CURSE ($7.95)
BULLDOG FAITH ($.75)
CHANGE YOUR LIFE ($.75)
CHILDREN WHO HIT THE MARK ($.75)
CONQUERING SETBACKS ($.75)
DAILY DEVOTIONAL ($5.95)
DEAR MARILYN ($6.95)
DIVORCE IS NOT THE ANSWER ($4.95)
EXPERIENCE LONG LIFE ($.75)
FASTING & PRAYER ($.75)
FREEDOM FROM BONDAGES ($4.95)
GIFT-WRAPPED FRUIT ($2.00)
GOD IN YOU, TO YOU, AND FOR YOU ($4.95)
GOD'S BENEFIT: HEALING ($.75)
GOD'S COVENANT FOR YOUR FAMILY ($4.95)
GOD'S RX FOR A HURTING HEART ($3.25)
GOD'S SEVEN KEYS TO MAKE YOU RICH ($.75)
HOLD ON TO YOUR DREAM ($.75)
HOW TO BECOME A MATURE CHRISTIAN ($5.95)
HOW TO BECOME MORE THAN A CONQUEROR ($.75)
HOW TO WIN FRIENDS ($.75)
I CAN BE BORN AGAIN AND SPIRIT FILLED ($.75)
I CAN DARE TO BE AN ACHIEVER ($.75)
KEYS TO HEALING REJECTION ($.75)
KNOW YOUR MINISTRY ($3.50)
MAXIMIZE YOUR DAY . . . GOD'S WAY ($7.95)
NAMES OF GOD ($7.95)
#1 KEY TO SUCCESS—MEDITATION ($2.50)
POWER OF FORGIVENESS, THE ($.75)
POWER OF THE BLOOD, THE ($.75)
RECEIVING RESURRECTION POWER ($.75)
RENEW YOUR MIND ($.75)
SATAN-PROOF YOUR HOME ($7.95)
SIGNS IN THE HEAVENS ($4.95)
SOLVING LIFE'S PROBLEMS ($.75)
SPEAK THE WORD ($.75)
STANDING IN THE GAP ($.75)
STORY OF ESTHER, THE ($.75)
WINNING OVER WEIGHT ($.75)
WOMEN OF THE WORD ($.75)
YOUR MIRACLE SOURCE ($2.50)
YOUR PERSONALITY WORKOUT ($7.95)

# PRAYER REQUEST

**Let us join our faith with yours for your prayer needs. Fill out below and send to**

Marilyn Hickey Ministries
P.O. Box 17340
Denver, CO 80217

Prayer Request _____

_____

_____

_____

_____

Name _____

Address_____

City_____

State_____ Zip_____

Phone (____) _____

☐ Please send me your free monthly magazine
   **OUTPOURING** (including daily devotionals,
   timely articles, and ministry updates).

☐ Please send me Marilyn's latest product catalog.

☐ Call our Prayer Center (303) 796-1333
   24 hours, 7 days a week.